REVISE PEARSON EDEXCEL GCSE (9–1)

History

EARLY ELIZABETHAN ENGLAND, 1558–88

PRACTICE PAPER Plus⁺

Series Consultant: Harry Smith

Author: Ben Armstrong

This Practice Paper is designed to complement your revision and to help you prepare for the exam. It does not include all the content and skills you need for the complete course and has been written to help you practise what you have learned. It may not be representative of a real exam paper. Remember that the official Pearson specification and associated assessment guidance materials are the only authoritative source of information and you should always refer to them for definitive guidance.

For further information, go to: **quals.pearson.com/GCSEHistory**

Contents

About this book

This book is designed to help you prepare for your Pearson Edexcel GCSE (9–1) History Early Elizabethan England, 1558–88 exam. It focuses on the skills you will need to answer the exam questions successfully.

You could work through the book in order. Alternatively, you could go straight to the section you want to focus on.

1 Knowledge booster

✓ Get started with these quick warm-up activities

✓ Recap what you already know about the topic

✓ Find out what you need to revise in more detail

✓ Use the links to the Revise Pearson Edexcel GCSE (9–1) History Revision Guide and Workbook to find more revision support

2 Exam skills

✓ Get useful tips and guidance on how the exam works and what you need to do

✓ Understand how each question type works

✓ See how to write a successful answer with the 'steps to success' skills builders

✓ Learn how to avoid common mistakes

This Practice Paper Plus book

3 Practice paper

✓ Write straight into this book

✓ Have a go at a full practice paper on this topic

✓ Use the hints and reminders in the margins to stay focused on what you need to do to answer each question successfully

✓ Tackle the paper under exam conditions by covering up the guidance in the margins

4 Practice paper answers

✓ Read the mark schemes and notes to find out what a successful answer would include

✓ See full example answers to each question

✓ Look at the annotations and comments to understand what makes each answer successful

✓ Get ideas about how to improve your own responses in the exam

Government and religion

This key topic is about the early years of Elizabeth's reign, from 1558 to 1569. It covers what England was like, how Elizabeth 'settled' religious problems and some of the challenges she faced.

Society and government in 1558

1 Complete this concept map with the main parts of Elizabeth's government. For each part, give the name and say what their role was.

Court – friends and advisers who influenced the queen's decisions

Elizabeth's government

Challenges at home and abroad in 1558

2 Complete this table about the challenges Elizabeth faced at home in 1558.

Challenge	Give **one** reason why this was a problem for Elizabeth
She was unmarried	
Her legitimacy was challenged	
The government had financial problems	

3 Which **three** countries were potential threats to Elizabeth?

....

Elizabeth's religious settlement of 1559

4 Draw lines to match the key terms on the left to the definitions on the right.

A. Act of Supremacy		**i.**	A set service to use in all churches
B. Book of Common Prayer		**ii.**	Instructions to priests on the new rules
C. Act of Uniformity		**iii.**	Law making all churches look the same and have the same services
D. Royal injunctions		**iv.**	Law making Elizabeth Head of the Church of England

Government and religion

Challenges to Elizabeth's religious settlement

5 Complete this table to show why and how Puritans and Catholics opposed the settlement.

	Puritans	Catholics
Two reasons why they opposed the settlement	• •	• •
One example of how they opposed the settlement		

The Catholic challenge from abroad

6 Give **three** reasons why Catholic countries opposed Elizabeth.

- ....
- ....
- ....

Why was Mary, Queen of Scots, a problem for Elizabeth?

7 State why Mary had a claim to the English throne.

....

8 Complete the table to show Elizabeth's possible solutions for Mary, and potential new problems.

Possible solution	Potential new problem
Hand Mary to Scottish lords	They might execute her, triggering war with France and Spain.
	There would be another Catholic ruler near England.
	Catholics in England might overthrow Elizabeth.
Send Mary abroad	

Revision Guide

How did you do? Go to pages 1–14 of the Revision Guide to remind yourself of any points you aren't sure about, and for more about this key topic.

Challenges to Elizabeth

This key topic is about the challenges Elizabeth faced at home and abroad later in her reign, from 1569 and 1588. It covers the plots and revolts in England, as well as the difficult relationship with Spain, which led to war and the Spanish Armada.

Plots and revolts against Elizabeth

1 Write numbers in the boxes to order these threats to Elizabeth from most serious (1) to least serious (4). Make sure you can give reasons for your choice.

☐ **A.** Revolt of the Northern Earls   ☐ **C.** Throckmorton Plot

☐ **B.** Ridolfi Plot   ☐ **D.** Babington Plot

2 Give **two** methods the spymaster Walsingham used to protect Elizabeth.

• ....

• ....

Mary's execution, 1587

3 Complete this concept map to give **four** reasons why Mary was executed.

Reasons for
execution

4 Give **two** reasons why Mary's execution was significant.

• ....

• ....

Rivalry with Spain

5 Decide which statements are true and which are false. Circle your answers.

		True	False
A.	Spain and England were happy to share trade in the New World.	True	False
B.	All trade in the New World had to be licensed by the Spanish government.	True	False
C.	Drake was ordered to avoid causing problems for the Spanish.	True	False
D.	To the Spanish, privateers like Drake were just pirates.	True	False
E.	Elizabeth supported the actions of the English privateers against Spain.	True	False

Challenges to Elizabeth

Relations with Spain

6 Complete the table below. Give **one** reason for each event.

Event	Why this made England's relationship with Spain worse
Dudley's campaign in the Netherlands, 1585–88	
Francis Drake's raid on the Spanish navy at Cadiz, 1587	

7 Which **one** of these sentences best describes the outcome of the English campaign in the Netherlands for England? Tick (✓) the correct answer.

A. A huge success ☐   **B.** A limited success ☐   **C.** A complete failure ☐

The Spanish Armada, 1588

8 Fill in the gaps to complete these sentences.

Philip II launched the Spanish Armada. The purpose was to attack ....

A main reason for this was that Philip wanted to put a .... on the throne

of England. The .... had promised absolution to anyone who supported

the Armada.

9 Which **one** of these sentences describes Philip's strategy? Tick (✓) the correct answer.

A. The Armada would sail straight to England and invade Kent. ☐

B. The Armada would collect soldiers from the Netherlands then invade Kent. ☐

C. The Armada would patrol the sea to stop England invading Spain. ☐

The English victory over the Spanish Armada

10 Which of the following are reasons why the English defeated the Armada? Tick (✓) the correct answers.

A. Communication problems ☐   **E.** The weather ☐

B. French ships helped England ☐   **F.** The Spanish gunpowder was wet ☐

C. English ships were better equipped ☐   **G.** English tactics were superior ☐

D. The Spanish panicked ☐   **H.** The Spanish were short of supplies ☐

Revision Guide

How did you do? Go to pages 15–25 of the Revision Guide to remind yourself of any points you aren't sure about, and for more about this key topic.

Society and exploration

This key topic is about Elizabethan society in the Age of Exploration, between 1558 and 1588. It covers education and leisure, the problem of the poor, and the exploration of the New World.

Education in Elizabethan England

1 (a) How did the nobility educate their children?

....

(b) Who attended grammar schools?

....

Entertainment in Elizabethan England

2 Complete this concept map with **five** examples of types of entertainment for each group.

For the lower classes — Elizabethan entertainment — For the nobility

The problem of the poor

3 Decide which statements are true and which are false. Circle your answers.

A. Poverty was not a serious problem in Elizabethan England.	True	False
B. Enclosure made poverty worse by fencing off common land.	True	False
C. Towns grew, which increased rents leading to greater poverty.	True	False
D. An increase in sheep farming meant more food for the poor.	True	False

4 Complete the table below with examples of policies toward the poor in Elizabethan England.

Law or action	How did it affect the poor?
Poor rate	
Charity	
	People who did not pay poor rates were punished.
1576 Poor Relief Act	
	Vagrants would be whipped and have a hole drilled through each ear. They could be executed for their third offence.

Society and exploration

Factors prompting exploration

5   Draw lines to match the reason for exploration on the left with the explanation on the right.

A. Expanding trade	**i.** The development of devices such as quadrants and astrolabes made voyages safer, more direct and faster.
B. New technology	**ii.** The wealthy were prepared to take risks for high profits, which made more voyages possible.
C. Adventure	**iii.** English traders needed to find new markets and products so travelled widely.
D. Triangular trade	**iv.** The method of buying and selling invented by John Hawkins encouraged other traders to work in a similar way.
E. Private investment	**v.** Accounts of riches found in distant lands encouraged young men to set sail on voyages of discovery.

Drake's circumnavigation of the globe

6   Which of the following are reasons why Drake set sail in 1577? Tick (✓) the correct answers.

   A. He wanted to sail around the globe. ☐

   B. He wanted to attack Spanish colonies in the Pacific. ☐

   C. He wanted revenge for a Spanish attack that had killed many of his men. ☐

   D. He had a bet with a Spanish captain that he could sail around the world. ☐

   E. He wanted the profits of trade from beyond the Americas. ☐

7   Give **two** reasons why Drake's circumnavigation was significant.

   •   ....

   •   ....

Raleigh and the attempted colonisation of Virginia

8   Give **one** reason why Raleigh's role in the attempted colonisation of Virginia was significant.

   ....

9   Give **two** reasons why the colonies in Virginia failed.

   •   ....

   •   ....

Revision Guide

How did you do? Go to pages 30–33 of the Revision Guide to remind yourself of any points you aren't sure about, and for more about this key topic.

In the exam

After all your revision and preparation, you want to do well. There are some key things you should remember in the exam.

What should I take with me?

- You must write in **black**, so it is a good idea to have more than one black pen with you.
- You might want a highlighter to mark the key words in the questions.
- Don't fill your desk with loads of other things. You know you won't need a calculator, for example, so leave it in your bag.
- Don't bother with correction fluid – just cross out any mistakes.

Where should I start?

Start with the front cover of your exam paper.

- The most important bit is the space for your name – don't forget to write it!
- It tells you how much time you have for the exam.
- For Paper 2, it will remind you to check you have both booklets (one for your period study and one for your British depth study).
- It will tell you which questions you **must** answer, and which ones you can choose.

How can I stay focused?

1. Take deep, slow breaths at the start of the exam, and to help you to focus as you work through the paper.
2. Highlight the key words in the questions, like dates, to make sure you focus on the right thing.
3. Plan your answers, especially for the longer essay questions. Work out what you want to say before you start writing.
4. If you get stuck, try a new question and come back to the other one later. Or make a list of what you do know about the topic in the question to help you get started.

How can I manage my time?

- It is a good idea to divide your time. Spend more time on questions that are worth more marks. You could even write on the paper (on the front cover or next to each question) the time you will start each question before you begin answering.
- Check the time regularly to make sure that you still have enough time for the longer answers.
- If you haven't finished answering a low-mark question but you are running out of time, move on to a higher-mark question. You can come back if you need to.

How much should I write?

- Your exam paper will give you space to write in for each question.
- Use the number of marks as a guide to how much you should write – a 12-mark question will need more than a 4-mark one.
- You don't always need to fill the space – this does not necessarily mean more marks.

How should I check my work?

Top tip

- Leave about five minutes at the end for checking.
- Check that you didn't miss any questions.
- Check your spelling and punctuation.
- Check that you have not made any obvious mistakes, like using the wrong date.

If you run out of space to finish an answer, **ask for more paper**. Don't use the answer space for the next question. This will make your answer hard to read. If you use extra paper, write 'answer on extra paper' at the bottom of the answer space. Then write the question number on the extra paper and complete your answer. At the end, check any extra paper has your name on it and that it is clear which answers you have finished there.

Had a look ☐ **Nearly there** ☐ **Nailed it!** ☐

Writing clear answers

The most important thing in the exam is writing the correct information, but it also helps to write clear, well-organised answers. This will make your answers easier to follow.

Get the basics right

✓ Use a good, **black** pen.

✓ Use paragraphs – they will help to make your points clearer.

✓ Write in the correct answer spaces. If you use extra paper, add a label to the new page to make it clear which question you are continuing. Write 'answer on extra paper' where you ran out of space.

✓ If you make a mistake, cross it out neatly.

How can I write clearly?

Paper 2 is not marked for spelling, punctuation and grammar, but you should still write well.

1 Always use formal language.

2 Use capital letters, full stops and commas correctly.

3 Connect ideas and make your meaning clear with phrases such as 'for example', 'however', 'consequently', 'significantly'.

4 Use key terms for the topic.

Does my handwriting matter?

Your work will be marked, no matter what your handwriting is like. **However**, it is always a good idea to write as neatly as you can to make sure all the words in your answer are clear.

Imagine you had to mark these sentences. Which is easiest to read?

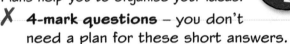

Should I plan my answers?

Plans help you to organise your ideas.

✗ **4-mark questions** – you don't need a plan for these short answers.

✓ **12-mark and 16-mark questions** – make a plan for these questions. Many of the best exam answers for these questions have plans.

There are different ways to plan. You can see examples on pages 18, 19, 22, 39, 43 and 47.

Top tip

How can I write effective paragraphs?

A good way to write effective paragraphs is to use **PEEL – Point, Evidence, Explain, Link:**

One reason that the Northern Earls revolted was to protect Catholicism. The Northern Earls had kept their Catholic faith after the religious settlement. Elizabeth had appointed a Protestant as Archbishop of Durham. The Northern Earls knew that Elizabeth wanted their Catholic religion to die out and they felt that they needed to fight to defend it. They also disliked the new archbishop. Therefore, the Earls prepared to revolt to protect Catholicism in England.

POINT – say what the paragraph is about.

EVIDENCE – give examples.

EXPLAIN – say what the evidence shows.

LINK – connect back to the question. This paragraph is answering the question 'Explain why the Northern Earls revolted in 1569'.

Had a look ☐   **Nearly there** ☐   **Nailed it!** ☐

Using key terms

Using key terms helps to show you know and understand the topic.

What key terms might I need to use?

accession – when a person becomes king or queen

auld alliance – a name used to describe the friendship between Scotland and France

Catholicism – the only type of Christianity followed in Western Europe until the 16th century. Catholics owe allegiance to the Pope, the head of the Catholic Church.

Church of England – the established church in England that became Protestant under Elizabeth

cipher – a code used to keep messages secret

circumnavigation (of the globe) – sailing all the way around (the world)

clergy – people who carry out religious duties

colonisation – when one country takes over another for its own use

court – all the advisers, friends and servants around a king or queen

divine right – the idea that God appointed monarchs (so they cannot be challenged)

deserving poor – people who were poor through no fault of their own and so were deserving of help

enclosure – when wealthy farmers closed off common farmland to use for themselves

idle poor – people who were poor due to laziness. The Elizabethans thought they did not deserve help

inflation – when money becomes worth less over time

legitimate (legitimacy) – born to parents who were married to each other

monarch – the king or queen

navigation – travelling (at this time by sea) from one place to another using maps and compasses

New World – the Elizabethan term for the Americas

papacy – the authority and power of the Pope

parliament – a group of politicians who pass laws and control taxes for the government. One half is the Commons and the other half the Lords.

Pope – the head of the Catholic Church.

privateers – armed ships owned and crewed by private individuals (also known as privateers) sent by the British government to attack foreign ships

Protestantism – a type of Christianity which began in Western Europe in the 16th century. Protestants do not accept the authority of the Pope or many of the teachings of the Catholic Church.

Puritan – a Protestant with very extreme religious beliefs

Privy Council – a group of advisers who helped the monarch to govern England

real wages – what a person's wages are worth in terms of what they can buy with the money

Reformation – when some churches in Europe, including the Church of England, changed from Catholic to Protestant

the slave trade – buying or kidnapping Africans and selling them as slave labour in the West Indies

vagabond (vagabondage) – a homeless beggar; the state of being a homeless beggar

vestments – the official clothes worn by clergy

Make sure that you can spell foreign or very old words, like **auld alliance**, correctly.

The key terms on this page are the most important ones. If you think of others, write them down in the back of this book.

The key terms with capital letters will always use capital letters, wherever they appear in a sentence.

Had a look ☐   **Nearly there** ☐   **Nailed it!** ☐

Understanding your exam

It is a good idea to understand how your exam works. You will know what to expect and this will help you to feel confident when you are in the exam.

Paper 2 British depth study

Your British depth study is one half of your Paper 2 exam. The other half is your period study. Paper 2 is...

✏️ a written exam

⏱️ 1 hour 45 minutes in total for both halves.

Your British depth study is...

⏱️ about 50 minutes

㉜ worth 32 marks

％ worth 20% of your GCSE History.

What will I get in the exam?

- You will get an exam paper. The paper has spaces to write your answers.
- Because Paper 2 has two halves, your exam paper will come as two booklets – one for your British depth study and one for your period study.
- You will be given both booklets at the same time.
- It is up to you which exam paper you do first – your British depth study or your period study.

What is a British depth study?

This paper – Early Elizabethan England, 1558–88 – explores a part of British history. It is called a depth study because the period of time it covers is quite a short one (1558–88), and it covers that time period in a lot of detail.

What historical skills does my Paper 2 British depth study assess?

Your GCSE History exam papers are designed to assess different historical skills, or 'Assessment Objectives' (AOs).

Your Paper 2 British depth study will assess these assessment objectives:

AO1 – Demonstrate knowledge and understanding of the key features of the period.

This means you need to show your knowledge of the topic, including details of the main events, people and themes.

AO2 – Explain and analyse events using second-order historical concepts.

This means you need to analyse historical ideas in your answers. These ideas are called **second-order historical concepts**.

Second-order concepts

- ✔️ Causation (why things happened)
- ✔️ Consequences (the results of something)
- ✔️ Similarity
- ✔️ Difference
- ✔️ Change
- ✔️ Continuity (staying the same)
- ✔️ Significance (how important an event, idea or change was)

Had a look ☐ **Nearly there** ☐ **Nailed it!** ☐

Understanding your exam

What type of questions will be on the exam paper for my British depth study?

The questions for your British depth study will always follow the same pattern:

1a Describe **two** features of ...

(4 marks)

Question 1a is the describing question:

(4) Worth 4 marks

Q Tests AO1

⏱ Spend about 6 minutes

✓ Describe **two** different features of the topic.

1b Explain why ...

(12 marks)

Question 1b is the explaining why question:

(12) Worth 12 marks

Q Tests AO1 and AO2

⏱ Spend about 18 minutes

✓ You get **two** prompts in the question and you **must** use some of your own information.

1c 'An opinion.' How far do you agree?

(16 marks)

Question 1c is the judgement question:

(16) Worth 16 marks

Q Tests AO1 and AO2

⏱ Spend about 24 minutes

✓ Pick **one of two** question choices

✓ You get **two** prompts in the question and you **must** use some of your own information

✓ You need to reach a judgement.

Had a look ☐ **Nearly there** ☐ **Nailed it!** ☐

Understanding Question 1a

Question 1a will always be structured in the same way. Make sure you know how this question works and what it is asking you to do.

How does Question 1a work?

This tells you that you need to write about **two** separate features.

> **1a** Describe **two** features of education in Elizabethan England.
>
> **(4 marks)**

Identify the command word. This question will always ask you to 'describe'.

Check how many marks the question is worth. This will help you to manage your time.

This is the topic for the question. Sometimes it will be broad like this, but it could be a specific event, like 'Drake's raid on Cadiz (1587)'.

Links This question is similar to Question 1 on Paper 1 (your thematic study).

What does Question 1a assess?

- ✓ Question 1a tests Assessment Objective 1.
- ✓ You need to show your knowledge of the topic.
- ✓ This will involve giving details of features such as main events, people and themes.

How long should I spend?

Spend about 6 minutes on Question 1a.

Try not to spend longer than this as the next questions will need plenty of time.

Take a look at page 10 for more about the assessment objectives.

What does 'describe' mean?

Describe means that your answer should show that you understand what the topic in the question is. You don't need to give reasons for it or say how important it was. You just need to give two separate pieces of information about the topic.

Top tip

The key thing to remember is that you can pick any two features but they **must** be connected to the topic in the question.

What is a feature?

A **feature** is a relevant piece of information about the topic. This could be what happened, who was involved, how it affected people or any other detail about the topic.

For example, for the question above about education, you could mention:
- who was educated
- where they were educated
- what they learned
- how education affected people
- attitudes to education.

Had a look ☐ **Nearly there** ☐ **Nailed it!** ☐

Understanding Question 1a

Features and supporting information

Each feature you describe in your answer needs supporting information. This means you need to give a bit more detail for each feature you identify. For example, for the question on education on page 12, you could have this feature and supporting information:

> One feature was that sons of nobles were often sent to other noble households to learn to become future noblemen.

This is a **valid feature** of Elizabethan education. This would get one mark.

> They would learn subjects like Latin and philosophy, but also horse riding and archery.

This is **supporting information** that adds to the feature about the education of noblemen. It is not a new feature. This would get one mark.

How is Question 1a marked?

Marks are available for identifying the features and for providing supporting information:

✓ There is **one mark available for each valid feature** you identify, so one mark for giving one feature and two marks for giving two features. Adding more features does not improve your mark.

✓ There is **one mark available** for adding supporting information to one of your features, and **two marks** if you add supporting information to both of your features.

Using language to write clear answers

To make your answer clear, you could introduce each feature like this:

> One feature was…
>
> A second feature was…

Top tip

> Remember to use **key terms** in your answer.

Turn to page 8 for more about writing clear answers. You can find examples of key terms on page 9.

Top tips for success

Top tip

✓ Describe **two different features** – take care not to use the same feature twice.

✓ Use **valid** features – make sure that both features are connected to the topic in the question.

✓ For each feature, write two sentences – one to **identify** the feature and one to add **supporting information** that is connected to that feature.

✓ Keep your answers **concise** – don't write more than you need to.

✓ **Use the space** on the exam paper – there will be a space marked for each feature.

✓ Be specific – avoid very general, vague sentences (like 'education was not very good').

✓ Be accurate – use correct facts to support your features.

Had a look ☐   **Nearly there** ☐   **Nailed it!** ☐

Answering Question 1a

You need to understand how you can write a successful answer to Question 1a.

Reading the question

> 1a Describe **two** features of education in Elizabethan England.
>
> **(4 marks)**

Always read the question carefully before you start writing your answer. Make sure you are clear about what the topic of the question is.

Short, 4-mark questions do not need a plan.

Steps to success

① Identify **one** valid feature of the topic. Write **one** sentence about it.

> Feature 1
>
> One feature was that middle-class boys were taught in grammar schools to be gentlemen.

Answer in the correct space on the page.

Describe your first feature in the space for 'Feature 1'.

Identify one valid feature that is relevant to the topic.

② **Add information** to support your first feature, using your knowledge of the topic. Write **one** sentence.

> This included learning Latin and how to debate.

Add a sentence of supporting information.

Make sure the supporting information is connected to your first feature. It should not be an unconnected fact.

③ Identify a **second** valid feature of the topic. Write **one** sentence about it.

> Feature 2
>
> A second feature was that boys and girls were educated separately.

Identify a second feature that is relevant to the topic.

Make sure your second feature is different to your first feature.

④ **Add information** to support your second feature, using your knowledge of the topic. Write **one** sentence.

> Boys learned more classical, academic subjects but education for girls was focused on the home and being mothers.

Add a sentence of supporting information.

Make sure the supporting information is connected to your second feature.

Had a look ☐ **Nearly there** ☐ **Nailed it!** ☐

Answering Question 1a

Getting it right

Question 1a should be a good chance to get some straightforward marks at the beginning of your exam paper. Stay focused on the question and don't write more than you need to. Look at these examples.

Feature 1

One feature was that there were strict punishments for students who broke the rules. **(1)** This could include being caned. **(1)**

Feature 2

A second feature was that the punishments were not pleasant. A student who broke the rules, like by being late, could be beaten.

✓ The first feature is valid – there were strict punishments. It also has relevant supporting information, which is an example of a punishment. So Feature 1 would get 2 marks.

✗ The second feature repeats the first feature, so does not get any marks. To improve, this answer needs a second feature that is different from the first.

✓ This is a valid feature.

Feature 1

Punishments in the schools were very harsh. **(1)** Young boys went to petty schools.

Feature 2

In grammar schools, boys often read parts of the Bible. **(1)** Sons of nobles learned things like dancing and wrestling.

✗ This supporting information is not connected to the feature so does not get any marks. The supporting information should be about the harsh punishments.

✗ This is also a valid feature, but again the supporting information is not connected to the feature so does not get any marks. It should be about using the Bible in school – for example, that many schools were run by Protestants.

Feature 1

One feature was that the children of yeomen would often learn through an apprenticeship. **(1)** This meant being trained by craftsmen to become a master at a specific job. **(1)**

Feature 2

A second feature was that most poor children did not go to school as they would grow up to be labourers. **(1)** This meant that most people in England did not learn to read or write. **(1)**

✓ This is a valid feature. It has also supporting information that develops the feature. So Feature 1 would get 2 marks.

✓ This is a second, different feature, which also has supporting information. So Feature 2 would get 2 marks.

Did you notice that the features in this strong answer are different from the ones in the answer on page 14? It doesn't matter which features you describe as long as they are accurate and valid.

Had a look ☐   **Nearly there** ☐   **Nailed it!** ☐

Understanding Question 1b

Question 1b will always be structured in the same way. Make sure you know how this question works and what it is asking you to do.

How does Question 1b work?

This is the issue that you need to explain.

If the question has dates, make sure that you write about the correct time period.

Identify the command phrase. This question will always ask you to 'explain why'.

You **must** include at least one reason from your own knowledge.

1b Explain why Elizabeth faced challenges to her authority when she became queen in 1558.

(12 marks)

You may use the following in your answer:

- financial problems
- the question of Elizabeth's legitimacy

You **must** also use information of your own.

Check how many marks the question is worth. This will help you to manage your time.

Look at the two suggestions. They might be helpful in deciding what to write about.

 Links This question is similar to Question 4 on Paper 1 (your thematic study) and Question 2 on Paper 3 (your modern depth study).

What does Question 1b assess?

- ☑ Question 1b tests Assessment Objectives 1 and 2.
- ☑ You need to show your knowledge of the topic.
- ☑ You also need to show you can explain and analyse **causation** (why events or changes happened).

How long should I spend?

Spend about 18 minutes on Question 1b.

This question is worth 12 marks so leave yourself enough time to do a good job. But don't spend too long – you will need enough time for the 16-mark essay question.

Take a look at page 10 for more about the assessment objectives.

What does 'explain why' mean?

Explaining why means giving reasons for something. It is different to just describing a topic. For example, if you were asked 'what was school like today?' you would describe your day. But if you were asked 'why did you go to school today?' you would give reasons why you went to school. It is the same with this question – you need to write an analysis that explains the issue in the question.

What will Question 1b focus on?

Question 1b could ask you about any aspect of Early Elizabethan England you have studied. It could be about a broad topic, like the example above (challenges to Elizabeth's authority), or a specific event, like Drake's raid on Cadiz (1587). The question could ask you to explain an event, a development, a success or a failure.

The key thing to remember is that you need **three reasons** and each one needs to be **connected** to the question topic.

 Top tip

Had a look ☐   **Nearly there** ☐   **Nailed it!** ☐

16

Understanding Question 1b

Choosing reasons

Question 1b will always include two bullet points. **These bullet points are only suggestions – you don't have to use them.** This type of question will always have several possible reasons. So if you don't know what one of the bullet points means, or you don't feel confident writing a paragraph about it, you can replace it with a reason of your own.

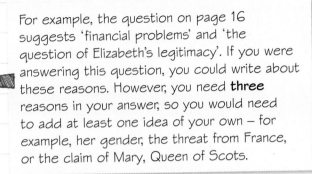

For example, the question on page 16 suggests 'financial problems' and 'the question of Elizabeth's legitimacy'. If you were answering this question, you could write about these reasons. However, you need **three** reasons in your answer, so you would need to add at least one idea of your own – for example, her gender, the threat from France, or the claim of Mary, Queen of Scots.

Remember!

Even if you replace one or both bullet points with another reason, you still need to give **three reasons** overall. At least one of the reasons needs to be your own information.

How is Question 1b marked?

Strong answers to Question 1b:

- ✓ Give an analytical explanation that is tightly focused on the question throughout.
- ✓ Keep the explanation clear and well organised throughout.
- ✓ Include information that is accurate, relevant and closely linked to the question.
- ✓ Show a wide range of knowledge and understanding of the topic.

Using language to write clear answers

To make your answer clear, you could start each paragraph like this:

> One reason was…
>
> A second reason was…
>
> A third reason was…

Writing analytically

You need to make sure you are **explaining why**. This is called writing analytically. Use phrases like these to explain the issue in the question:

- This led to…
- As a result…
- Consequently…
- This increased/reduced…
- This showed that…

Top tip

Remember to use **key terms** in your answer.

Turn to page 8 for more about writing clear answers. You can find examples of key terms on page 9.

You don't need to write an introduction or a conclusion for Question 1b.

Top tips for success

Top tip

- ✓ Give **three reasons** in your explanation.
- ✓ Include **information of your own**.
- ✓ **Plan** your answer before you write. This will help you to stay focused on the question throughout your answer.
- ✓ Structure your answer clearly using **PEEL paragraphs**.
- ✓ **Explain clearly** why each reason you include explains the issue in the question.
- ✓ Support each reason with **clear and accurate information** about the topic.
- ✓ If the question includes a date range (for example, 'between 1558 and 1588'), only include information from that period.

Had a look ☐ **Nearly there** ☐ **Nailed it!** ☐

Answering Question 1b

You need to understand how you can write a successful answer to Question 1b.

Reading the question

> **1b** Explain why Elizabeth faced <u>challenges to her authority</u> when she became queen in 1558.
>
> **(12 marks)**
>
> You may use the following in your answer:
>
> - financial problems
> - the question of Elizabeth's legitimacy
>
> You **must** also use information of your own.

Always read the question carefully before you start writing your answer. Make sure you are clear on the topic.

Check the number of marks. This will help you to use your time well in the exam.

How can I structure my answer?

1 Write about your first reason in one PEEL paragraph.

2 Write about your second reason in one PEEL paragraph.

3 Write about your third reason in one PEEL paragraph.

Remember **PEEL**: Point – Evidence – Explain – Link.

You can find out more about paragraphing and the PEEL structure on page 8.

Plan your answer

This question is worth 12 marks, so take a minute or two to make a quick plan before you start writing.

> 1. <u>Financial problems</u>
>   - £300 000 debt
>   - expensive wars
>   - bad harvests
> 2. The question of Elizabeth's legitimacy
>   - Catholics denied Henry VIII's annulment
>   - <u>Mother = executed</u>
> 3. <u>Gender</u>
>   - Sister 'Bloody' Mary
>   - Pressure to marry but would lose power

The best answers are well organised, with three paragraphs. Structure your plan to reflect this.

Number the points in your plan so you have an order for your answer.

Keep your plan short and simple. You don't need to write in full sentences.

Remember to include your own knowledge in the plan. This plan includes a third reason that was not mentioned in the question.

This is one style of plan. You can see another style on page 39.

Had a look ☐ **Nearly there** ☐ **Nailed it!** ☐

Answering Question 1b

Steps to success

1 Write a paragraph about your first point. Remember to use PEEL to structure your paragraph clearly.

One reason that Elizabeth faced challenges to her authority was that she had financial problems. When she was crowned, the government was £300 000 in debt, which was more than the income received from taxes in a year. This was the result of bad harvests and expensive wars before she became queen. Consequently, Elizabeth's funds were low. This presented a challenge to Elizabeth's authority because without enough money it was hard for her to govern the country or to pay for important things, like soldiers if England was attacked.

Make a clear **point** at the start to show what the paragraph is about. This example uses one of the reasons given in the question.

Include some **evidence**. This example only uses a couple of points but it is enough to show understanding of the topic.

Explain how the reason caused the consequence (a challenge).

Link back to the question. This example uses words from the question to make the link.

2 Write a paragraph about your second point. Keep focused on the question and use PEEL to structure your writing.

A second reason was the question of Elizabeth's legitimacy. Elizabeth had been born to Henry VIII's second wife, Anne Boleyn. Although the marriage was legal in English law, many Catholics refused to accept the annulment of Henry's first marriage under Church law. Catholics claimed that the new marriage was not legal, which would mean that Elizabeth was illegitimate and could not be queen. Henry had even declared her illegitimate after Anne's execution. This presented Elizabeth with a challenge to her authority because it meant that her opponents could claim that she did not have any right to be the queen of England.

Point

Evidence

Explain – here, the phrase 'which would mean' is used to write analytically.

Link back to the question.

3 Write a paragraph about your third point. Remember to refer back to your plan and stay focused on explaining why.

A third reason was her gender. Like her sister Mary, Elizabeth was female...

As a result...

This challenged Elizabeth's authority because...

Always include **three** reasons. This paragraph is about a reason that was not suggested in the question, so it also uses your own knowledge.

Had a look ☐   **Nearly there** ☐   **Nailed it!** ☐

Understanding Question 1c

Question 1c will always be structured in the same way. Make sure you know how this question works and what it is asking you to do.

How does Question 1c work?

Identify the opinion in the statement. This question will always start with an opinion about something.

Identify the command phrase. 'How far' means you need to make a judgement. You also need to explain and justify your judgement.

Look at the two factors suggested. They might be helpful in deciding what to write about.

> **1c** 'The main reason for the increase in exploration by 1588 was new technology.'
>
> How far do you agree? Explain your answer.
>
> **(16 marks)**
>
> You may use the following in your answer:
>
> • new navigation technology
>
> • wealth
>
> You **must** also use information of your own.

Check how many marks the question is worth. This will help you to manage your time.

You **must** use your own information. This includes writing about at least one factor that is not given in the question.

 Links This question is similar to Question 5/6 on Paper 1 (your thematic study).

In the exam, you will have **a choice of two questions** for Question 1c. Both of them will be structured like this example.

What does Question 1c assess?

✓ Question 1c tests Assessment Objectives 1 and 2.

✓ You need to show your knowledge of the topic.

✓ You also need to show you can explain and analyse events using second-order concepts such as causation and change.

How long should I spend?

Spend about 24 minutes on Question 1c.

This question is worth more marks than any other question on your exam paper, so leave enough time to finish your answer.

Take a look at page 10 for more about the assessment objectives.

Analysing the statement

• **Identify what the question is about.** The example above is about 'the increase in exploration by 1588'.

• **Identify the opinion clearly.** In the example above, the opinion is that new technology was more important than other factors for the increase in exploration.

Choosing factors to write about

Question 1c will always include two bullet points. **These bullet points are only suggestions of factors you could use to support or challenge the statement – you don't have to use them.** If you don't know what one of the bullet points means, or you don't feel confident writing about it, you can choose to write about another factor.

Had a look ☐   **Nearly there** ☐   **Nailed it!** ☐

Understanding Question 1c

'How far do you agree?'

You need to make a judgement about the statement in the question.

Top tip

- Look at evidence that agrees with the statement **and** at evidence that challenges it.
- Use your knowledge to reach an overall judgement – don't just write down everything you know about the topic.
- Explain why you have made that judgement.

Constructing an overall judgement

Your overall judgement needs to be justified – you need to include a reason for your decision. In your overall judgement, make sure you:

- **Say how far you agree** with the statement – for example, 'Overall, I agree ...'
- **Give a clear reason** for your opinion. Say why you have reached this decision by comparing the factors in a short summary at the end of your answer.

How is Question 1c marked?

Strong answers to Question 1c:

- ✓ Give an analytical explanation that is tightly focused on the question throughout.
- ✓ Keep their explanation clear and well organised throughout.
- ✓ Include information that is accurate, relevant and closely linked to the question.
- ✓ Show a wide range of knowledge and understanding of the topic.
- ✓ Reach an overall judgement that is fully justified.

You **will** need to write an introduction and conclusion for Question 1c.

Writing analytically

Use phrases that show you are **explaining** the opinion in the statement and making a judgement about that viewpoint. This is called writing analytically. For example:

- I agree/disagree...
- Although I agree to a certain extent... it is also true that...
- The viewpoint in the statement is valid because...
- This can be supported by...

Top tip

Remember to use **key terms** in your answer.

Turn to page 8 for more about writing clear answers. You can find examples of key terms on page 9.

Top tips for success

- ✓ Start with a **short introduction**. Say what you are going to write about in your answer.
- ✓ Include **arguments for the statement** and **counter-arguments** (arguments against it).
- ✓ Use **clear and accurate evidence** to support your arguments.
- ✓ **Explain clearly why** your evidence supports or challenges the statement.
- ✓ **Link factors together and compare them** to say which is more important.
- ✓ Use **your own information**, including at least one factor not in the question.
- ✓ End with a **conclusion**. Make an **overall judgement** about how far you agree with the statement.
- ✓ **Plan** your answer before you write to help you stay focused on the question.
- ✓ Structure your answer clearly using **PEEL paragraphs**.
- ✓ If the question includes a date range, only include information from that period.

Had a look ☐   **Nearly there** ☐   **Nailed it!** ☐

Answering Question 1c

You need to understand how you can write a successful answer to Question 1c.

Reading the question

> **1c** 'The main reason for the increase in exploration by 1588 was new technology.'
>
> How far do you agree? Explain your answer.
>
> **(16 marks)**
>
> You may use the following in your answer:
>
> • new navigation technology
>
> • wealth
>
> You **must** also use information of your own.

Always read the question carefully before you start writing your answer.

Make sure you identify the opinion in the statement.

Use **PEEL** paragraphs: **Point – Evidence – Explain – Link.**

You can find out more about paragraphing and the PEEL structure on page 8.

How can I structure my answer?

1 Write a short introduction. Say what the question is about and what you will write about.

2 Begin your argument. You could start by writing about evidence that supports the statement.

3 Continue your argument. If you started with evidence that supports the statement, move on to write about other factors that challenge the statement.

4 Write a conclusion. Give an overall judgement and explain why you reached that decision.

Plan your answer

This question is worth 16 marks, so take the time to make a good plan before you start writing.

Support	Challenge
1. New nav. tech.	1. Wealth
• Astrolabes	• Triangular trade
• Quadrants	• New resources
2. Better ships	2. Adventure
• Sails	• Drake's stories
• Strength	• Printing press for
• More guns	sharing stories
Judgement: Wealth more impt. – £ needed for tech.	

The best answers are structured logically. In your plan, list factors that support and challenge the statement.

Add specific evidence and facts so you remember to use them.

Include your own knowledge. This factor was not mentioned in the question.

Include a judgement in the plan to help you stay focused.

Had a look ☐   **Nearly there** ☐   **Nailed it!** ☐

Answering Question 1c

Steps to success

1 Write a short introduction. Say what the question is about and what you will write about in your answer.

> There were several reasons why there was an increase in exploration by 1588. One was that there was new technology. However, I disagree that this was the main reason. There were other reasons, such as people's desire to get rich, and a sense of adventure. The biggest reason was the desire for wealth.

Identify what the question is about. You can use the words from the statement.

Indicate the viewpoints that you will cover in the question.

Make a judgement. You don't have to do this here but it will help to focus your answer if you do.

2 Begin your argument. You could start by writing about evidence that supports the statement, as in this example. Use PEEL paragraphs to make your writing clear and well organised.

> New technology did contribute to the increase in exploration. This can be supported by the new types of navigation equipment which were invented. Sailors could now use astrolabes and quadrants. These were important because they allowed sailors to work out where they were, so they could sail in a more accurate direction and get to their destination more easily. This made sailing faster and safer, so more people took the risk of exploring.

Use clear language to identify the **point**.

Use your knowledge to give **evidence**. These are two **specific** examples.

Explain how your evidence supports your point. Here, the phrase 'These were important because' is used to write analytically.

Link back to the question.

3 Continue your argument. If you started with evidence that supports the statement, move on to write about other factors, as in this example. Use PEEL paragraphs.

> Although I agree with the viewpoint in the statement to an extent, there were other important factors. The desire for adventure was an important cause of increased exploration. Once new technology had improved sailing, many people...

Use phrases that show you are writing analytically – making a judgement about the viewpoint in the statement.

Always include a **counter-argument**, even if your overall judgement is that you agree with the statement.

Link factors together. This shows the connection between technology and adventure.

Remember to include information that is not given in the question. This factor was not in the question.

4 Write a conclusion. Give an overall judgement about how far you agree with the statement. Explain why you reached that decision.

> Overall, I disagree with the statement. Wealth was the main reason for the increase of exploration. New technology did make exploring faster and safer, so it became more common. But the reason for creating the technology was that merchants and privateers wanted to make profits from sailing to the New World. Therefore the desire for wealth was a motive for the technology and this makes wealth a more important reason.

Start your conclusion clearly – **give your overall judgement** on the statement. You could also start with 'In conclusion...'

Explain your overall judgement by comparing the factor in the statement to the other factors you have considered.

Had a look ☐   **Nearly there** ☐   **Nailed it!** ☐

This is how long you have to answer all the questions for your Paper 2 British depth study **and** your Paper 2 period study in the exam.

Paper 2 is split into two booklets: booklet B for your British depth study (like this one) and booklet P for your period study.

Get used to writing with a **black** pen.

In the exam, there will be spaces for you to do this.

Check carefully which questions you must answer, and where you have a choice.

Focus on answering each question fully, rather than trying to fill all the writing lines.

Pearson Edexcel GCSE (9–1)

History

Paper 2: Period study and British depth study

Booklet B4: Early Elizabethan England, 1558–88

Time: 1 hour 45 minutes (Total time for **both** booklets)

You must have: The corresponding booklet P

Instructions

- Use **black** ink or ball-point pen
- **Fill in** your name, centre number and candidate number.
- There are two booklets in this question paper. **This is booklet B. Answer questions 1a, 1b and either 1c(i) or 1c(ii) from this booklet.**
- Answer the questions in the spaces provided – there may be more space than you need.

Information

- The total mark for this booklet is 32.
- The total time for **both** booklets is 1 hour 45 minutes.
- The marks for **each** question are shown in brackets.

Try to divide the time equally between your British depth study and your period study. Your period study is also worth 32 marks.

Use the marks to help you work out how long to spend on each question.

Top tip

Make sure you:

- read each question carefully before you start writing your answer
- try to answer every question
- save about five minutes to check your answers at the end.

Answer Question 1a, Question 1b and EITHER Question 1c(i) OR Question 1c(ii).

1a Describe **two** features of Elizabeth's government when she became queen (1558).

(4 marks)

Feature 1

....

....

....

....

....

....

Feature 2

....

....

....

....

....

....

Time

Spend **about 6 minutes** on this question.

Unlocking the question

'**Describe**' means giving information. You don't need to give reasons.

Unlocking the question

A **feature** means any relevant, accurate piece of information about the topic.

Revision Guide

Revise this topic on page 1.

Watch out!

Make sure you describe **two different features**.

Hint

Add supporting details to **each** feature.

Watch out!

Make sure that your supporting information is **connected** to the feature.

Hint

Use language such as 'One feature was...' to make your answer clear. Use **key terms**.

Top tip

Be specific, accurate and keep your answers short.

Time

Spend **about 18 minutes** on this question.

Top tip

Always start 12-mark questions with a quick **plan**. Use the Notes pages at the back of this book if you need extra space, but keep your plan **short**.

Unlocking the question

'**Explain why**' means giving reasons for something.

Unlocking the question

You need to give **three reasons**. You can use the bullet points in the question if you want to, but you don't have to.

Watch out!

Even if you replace the bullet points with your own ideas, you still need three reasons overall.

Watch out!

You **don't** have to decide which reason was more important.

Unlocking the question

You **must** include at least one reason from your own knowledge.

Revision Guide

Revise this topic on pages 10–12.

1b Explain why there was opposition to Elizabeth's religious settlement (1559).

(12 marks

You may use the following in your answer:

- Puritan opposition
- foreign powers

You **must** also use information of your own.

....

....

....

....

....

....

....

....

....

....

....

....

....

....

....

....

....

....

....

....

....

....

....

....

....

....

....

....

....

....

....

....

....

....

....

....

....

....

....

....

....

....

....

....

....

....

....

....

....

....

....

....

....

....

....

....

....

Unlocking the question

You do not need to write an introduction or a conclusion in this answer.

LEARN IT!

Structure your answer clearly. Use a separate **PEEL (Point – Evidence – Explain – Link)** paragraph to write about each reason.

Hint

Clearly **signpost your reasons** using language such as 'One reason was...', 'A second reason was...'

Hint

Support each reason with clear and accurate information about the topic.

LEARN IT!

Use phrases like 'as a result...', 'consequently...' or 'this caused...' to focus your answer and show you are writing analytically.

Watch out!

Make sure that you are giving reasons for the issue in the question, not just describing the topic. You need to say clearly why each reason you give caused the consequence in the question.

Hint

Use **key terms**, like names, dates or specific example, to support each reason you give.

Aim higher

Make sure your explanation is analytical and keep it tightly focused on the question **throughout** your answer.

....
....
....
....
....
....
....
....
....
....
....
....
....
....
....
....
....
....
....
....
....
....
....
....
....
....
....
....
....
....
....

Answer EITHER Question 1c(i) OR Question 1c(ii).

EITHER

1c(i) 'The greatest danger to Elizabeth in the years 1569–88 was the threat of assassination.'

How far do you agree? Explain your answer.

(16 marks)

You may use the following in your answer:

- the Babington Plot
- the Spanish Armada

You **must** also use information of your own.

OR

1c(ii) 'The main consequence of Drake's circumnavigation of the globe was to damage England's relationship with Spain.'

How far do you agree? Explain your answer.

(16 marks)

You may use the following in your answer:

- attacks on Spanish colonies
- encouraging exploration in the New World

You **must** also use information of your own.

Time

Remember that this question is worth more marks than the other questions on your British depth study. Make sure you leave enough time to answer it fully.

Watch out!

In the exam, you should only answer **either** Question 1c(i) **or** Question 1c(ii). In this practice paper there is space for you to have a go at both options.

Hint

Look carefully at each option, including the suggestions in the bullet points and consider how much you know about each topic. Choose the option you feel you are most confident writing about.

Revision Guide

For Question 1c(i), revise dangers to Elizabeth on pages 15–19 and 23–24.

Revision Guide

For Question 1c(ii), revise Drake's circumnavigation on page 31.

Hint

Use this space to answer Question 1c(i).

Time

Spend **about 24 minutes** on this question.

Top tip

Always start 16-mark questions with a good **plan**. Include factors that support and counter the statement in the question.

Unlocking the question

Identify the opinion in the statement before you start writing.

Hint

Start with a short introduction. Summarise the question and what you will mention in the answer.

Aim higher

State your judgement in the introduction. It will help you to keep your answer focused.

Top tip

Structure your answer clearly. Either start by writing about information that supports the statement or information that challenges it.

Indicate which question you are answering by marking a cross in the box ☒. If you change your mind, put a line through the box ☒ and then indicate your new question with a cross ☒.

Chosen question number:

Question 1c(i) ☒

Question 1c(ii) ☒

....
....
....
....
....
....
....
....
....
....
....
....
....
....
....
....
....
....
....
....
....
....
....
....
....

....

....

....

....

....

....

....

....

....

....

....

....

....

....

....

....

....

....

....

....

....

....

....

....

....

....

....

....

....

....

....

....

....

....

....

....

....

....

....

Unlocking the question

You need to reach a clear **judgement** in your answer.

Unlocking the question

You don't have to use the two bullet points but they might help you decide what to write about.

Unlocking the question

You **must** include information from your own knowledge. Make sure you include at least one factor that is not mentioned in the question.

Unlocking the question

It doesn't matter whether you agree or disagree with the statement. Your answer still needs to consider evidence that supports the statement **and** evidence that challenges it.

Aim higher

It is a good idea to link the factors together. One place to do this is in the conclusion but you can do it earlier as well.

Watch out!

Stick to the time period the question is asking about.

Watch out!

Stay focused. Link each point of evidence back to the question.

Hint

Link each point of evidence back to the question. You could use phrases like 'this shows that...' or 'this is evidence that...'.

Aim higher

Include **specific** details, such as examples of people, events and dates, to back up each point.

Aim higher

You don't need to wait until the conclusion to give your judgement. As you write about a factor, use phrases like 'this was more/less important because...' to show your viewpoint.

Hint

Use **key terms** to show your knowledge of the topic.

Top tip

Use PEEL **(Point – Evidence – Explain – Link)** paragraphs to organise each main point.

LEARN IT!

Use language to show you are **analysing**, such as 'this meant that...', 'the effect of this was...', 'this increase shows...' or 'this demonstrates that...'.

....

....

....

....

....

....

....

....

....

....

....

....

....

....

....

....

....

....

....

....

....

....

....

....

....

....

....

....

....

....

....

....

....

Hint

Keep your points **specific** and **accurate**.

Watch out!

Don't just describe the topic. You need to reach a judgement on **how far** you agree with the statement, so be clear about how your examples support or challenge the statement.

Hint

Remember that you need a conclusion that reaches a clear judgement.

Hint

You could start your conclusion with 'Overall, I…' or 'In conclusion…'.

Watch out!

State how far you agree with the statement **and** explain why you have reached this judgement.

Top tip

Think about why you have reached your judgement. Did a factor have more effect than other factors? Did it involve more people? Did it last longer, or start earlier? Did one factor cause other factors?

Aim higher

Link the factors together in your conclusion.

Hint

Use this space to answer Question 1c(ii).

Time

Spend **about 24 minutes** on this question.

Top tip

Always start 16-mark questions with a good **plan** to help you organise your ideas.

Top tip

In your plan, list factors that support the statement in the question and list factors that go against the statement.

Unlocking the question

Look at the two bullet points. They will help you decide what to include in your answer.

Aim higher

Decide on your judgement **before** you start writing. This will help you to write a more focused analytical explanation.

Hint

Start with an introduction. Give a short summary of what you will write about.

**Indicate which question you are answering by marking a cross in the box ☒.
If you change your mind, put a line through the box ☒ and then indicate your new question with a cross ☒.**

Chosen question number:

Question 1c(i) ☒
Question 1c(ii) ☒

....
....
....
....
....
....
....
....
....
....
....
....
....
....
....
....
....
....
....
....
....
....
....
....

....

....

....

....

....

....

....

....

....

....

....

....

....

....

....

....

....

....

....

....

....

....

....

....

....

....

....

....

....

....

....

....

....

....

....

....

....

....

....

....

....

Unlocking the question

You **must** include information from your own knowledge. Include at least one factor that is not mentioned in the question.

Unlocking the question

It doesn't matter whether you agree or disagree with the statement. You must still consider evidence that supports the statement **and** evidence that challenges it.

Top tip

Start each paragraph with **clear language** that focuses what you are writing. For example, you could write, 'Another example that supports/challenges the statement is…'.

Watch out!

Stay focused. Link each point of evidence back to the question to avoid going off the topic.

Aim higher

Include **specific, accurate details** to back up each main point.

Hint

Once you have written about your evidence that supports or challenges the statement, write your **counter-argument** – the opposite viewpoint.

Top tip

Write **analytically**. Show you are explaining your judgement by using phrases like 'this shows that...', 'this was important because...', 'the consequence of this was...' or 'subsequently...'.

Watch out!

Make sure you stick to the time period the question is asking about.

Watch out!

You need to **explain why** your evidence supports or challenges the statement. Don't just describe what you know.

Aim higher

You don't need to wait until the conclusion to show your judgement. As you write about a factor, use phrases like 'this was more/ less important because...' to explain your viewpoint.

Top tip

Use PEEL **(Point – Evidence – Explain – Link)** paragraphs to organise each main point.

Top tip

As you write, look back at the question occasionally. This will help you to stay focused on the question.

....

....

....

....

....

....

....

....

....

....

....

....

....

....

....

....

....

....

....

....

....

....

....

....

....

....

....

....

....

....

....

Hint

Always finish Question 1c with a conclusion that gives an **overall judgement** that is fully justified.

Hint

You could start your conclusion with 'Overall, I…' or 'In conclusion…'.

Watch out!

Don't just give your opinion. Make sure you **explain why** you have reached your judgement.

Top tip

Double-check your conclusion. What reason have you given for your judgement? Make sure it is clear and specific.

**Answer Question 1a, Question 1b and EITHER
Question 1c(i) OR Question 1c(ii).**

1a Describe **two** features of Elizabeth's government when she became queen (1558).

(4 marks)

Feature 1

A valid feature of Elizabeth's government.

One feature of Elizabeth's government was the Privy Council. This was made up of advisers to the queen who met at least three times per week to help her govern.

Additional information gives more detail about the feature (the Privy Council).

Answer is kept concise with specific and accurate examples given.

Each feature is written in the space provided.

Feature 2

A second feature of the government was that it was advised by Parliament. There were two parts: the House of Commons that was elected, and the House of Lords, which was made up of noblemen.

Second feature is different to the first and is also valid.

Second feature is also developed with accurate supporting information.

Alternative answers

Answers to Question 1a could also include:

• The role of Elizabeth as monarch. **(1)** She ruled by 'divine right'. **(1)**
• The lords lieutenant. **(1)** They represented the government in each county of England. **(1)**
• The Justices of the Peace. **(1)** They were landowners who kept law and order in the local area. **(1)**
• The royal court. **(1)** They were friends and advisers of the queen who could influence her decisions. **(1)**

1b Explain why there was opposition to Elizabeth's religious settlement (1559).

(12 marks)

You may use the following in your answer:

- Puritan opposition
- foreign powers

You **must** also use information of your own.

Hint

Read the notes below, then look at the sample answer that follows.

Writing a good answer

Good answers will:

- give an analytical explanation that is tightly focused on the question throughout
- keep explanations clear and well organised throughout
- include information that is accurate, relevant and closely linked to the question
- show a wide range of knowledge and understanding of the topic.

Relevant points may include:

- Puritans were offended by Catholic features of the settlement.
- Catholics objected to the religion being an officially Protestant church.
- Foreign Catholic nations in conflict with Britain saw it as their duty to restore Catholicism to England.
- The Pope ordered Catholics to not support the Church of England.
- Many individual Catholics, called recusants, refused to go to services.
- Wealthy Catholic families continued to hold Catholic services.

Q1b: sample answer

Plan:

Counter-Reformation   Pope's instruction 1566   Crucifixes   Vestments

Catholic opposition   Puritan opposition

Opposition to the 1559 religious settlement

Foreign powers' opposition

France + Spain were Catholic

Hint

Look at this sample answer to Question 1b. Refer back to the notes above, then look to see how some of the points are used.

Quick plan helps to keep answer clear and focused.

Paragraph starts with a point that is focused on the question.

PEEL used to give clear structure in every paragraph.

Specific, accurate knowledge used to support points. This, for example, does not just say that Puritans did not like the settlement.

Answer is clear and well organised.

Answer tightly focused on question throughout.

Shows a wide range of knowledge and understanding of topic.

One reason that there was opposition to Elizabeth's religious settlement was that Puritans objected to the Catholic elements. Elizabeth tried to make each church have a crucifix, but Puritans saw these as idols that would offend God. Some Puritan bishops threatened to resign in response to the religious settlement, and Elizabeth backed down on the crosses. She also insisted that all priests should wear special vestments, like Catholic priests. This led to the resignation of 37 Puritan priests in protest. The Puritans thought the Church of England Elizabeth created in the settlement was too Catholic, and as a result they opposed the settlement.

A second reason for opposition came from foreign powers. Spain and France were strongly Catholic, so they opposed the Protestant elements of the religious settlement anyway. But Elizabeth supported Protestant lords in Scotland to rebel against Mary, Queen of Scots, who was half French. Then she supported Protestants in France who were revolting against the king. She allowed Protestant rebels from the Netherlands to flee to England and even used English harbours to attack Spanish ships. As a result, France and Spain saw their problems with England as a struggle between Protestantism and Catholicism, and opposed Elizabeth's settlement.

Language used to show writing is analytical – shows answer is explaining why.

Includes own knowledge – a third reason, which was not given in the question.

A third reason why there was opposition was the influence of the Pope. The Pope encouraged Catholics in England not to support the religious settlement. In 1566, he gave an instruction that they should not go to Church of England services. Catholics who continued to practise their religion were called recusants. Elizabeth instructed the authorities not to investigate recusants very closely because she did not want to make them into martyrs by punishing them. Consequently, many Catholics were able to follow the Pope's instruction by refusing to support the religious settlement.

Includes specific and accurate examples and explains why these led to opposition.

Key term used to show detailed knowledge of topic.

Language used shows writing is analytical throughout the answer.

A very strong answer because...

This answer is focused on the question all the way through. It gives three different and very clear reasons why there was opposition to the religious settlement. Each reason is supported by detailed, accurate and relevant information. The answer includes detailed own knowledge. There is one, clear paragraph for each point and a clear explanation of why each reason given caused opposition to the religious settlement.

Hint

Read the notes below, then look at the sample answer on pages 43–45.

Hint

Remember – in the exam you only need to answer **either** Question 1c(i) **or** Question 1c(ii).

1c(i) 'The greatest danger to Elizabeth in the years 1569–88 was the threat of assassination.'

How far do you agree? Explain your answer.

(16 marks)

You may use the following in your answer:

- the Babington Plot
- the Spanish Armada

You **must** also use information of your own.

Writing a good answer

Good answers will:

- give an analytical explanation that is tightly focused on the question throughout
- keep explanations clear and well organised throughout
- include information that is accurate, relevant and closely linked to the question
- show a wide range of knowledge and understanding of the topic
- reach an overall judgement that is fully justified.

Relevant points that support the statement may include:

- The Ridolfi Plot (1571) included plans for Ridolfi to assassinate Elizabeth and replace her with Mary, Queen of Scots. It was a real threat to Elizabeth's life as it had the support of the Pope and the French king.
- The Babington Plot (1586) was another assassination plot, involving six Catholics, the Pope, the King of France, the King of Spain, and Mary, Queen of Scots, herself. It was a real danger to Elizabeth's life.

Relevant points that counter the statement may include:

- There was the threat from the Catholic nobility, especially in the North, who opposed the religious settlement.
- There was the threat of revolt supported by French invasion with the Throckmorton Plot.
- There was a threat of foreign invasion from the Spanish Armada (1588).

Effective plan helps to keep answer clear, well structured and focused throughout.

Hint

Look at this sample answer to Question 1c(i). Refer back to the notes on page 42, then look to see how some of the points are used here.

Q1c(i): sample answer

Plan:

Support	Challenge
Threats of assassination:	Revolts:

1. Ridolfi Plot
   • 1571
   • Plot with Duke of Norfolk
	3. Northern Earls
	   • Catholic revolt
	   • Lasted a month

2. Babington Plot
   • 1586
   • 6 Catholics involved
   • Mary definitely involved
	4. Throckmorton
	   • Plan to remove Elizabeth and invite French invasion
	
	5. Invasion: Spanish Armada
	   • 1588
	   • Spanish had beaten English in Netherlands

Judgement – Invasion was bigger threat as the plots were stopped before threatening Elizabeth.	

Including a judgement in a plan helps keep the whole answer focused.

Introduction kept short and simple.

Between 1569 and 1588, Elizabeth faced many dangers. One was the threat of assassination, but she also faced revolts from Catholics in England. Although I agree to an extent that this was a potential danger, it is also true that she faced bigger dangers, such as invasion by France or Spain.

Sticks to the dates given in question.

Language used shows writing is analytical and gives a judgement.

In this period, the threat of assassination was a real danger to Elizabeth. This can be supported by the Ridolfi Plot of 1571. An Italian banker called Ridolfi plotted to assassinate Elizabeth and replace her with Mary, Queen of Scots, who would marry the Duke of Northumberland. The viewpoint in the statement is valid because the Ridolfi Plot was a real danger to Elizabeth because the plan had the support of the Pope, as well as the support of the King of France who ordered 10 000 men to be ready to invade if Elizabeth was assassinated. Therefore there was the potential for Elizabeth to be killed, which shows that the threat of assassination was real.

Paragraph starts with a point focused on the question.

Uses own knowledge, not given in question.

Includes specific examples of accurate evidence.

Introduction sums up the question and says what the answer will discuss.

43

Language clearly signposts second example of assassination will be discussed.

Links back to question.

Shows detailed knowledge and understanding of a factor given in the question.

Another example that supports the view in the statement that assassination was a real danger to Elizabeth was the Babington Plot of 1586. This was a plot by six Catholics, including Babington, to murder Elizabeth and put Mary on the throne. The plot was supported by the King of France, the King of Spain and also the Pope. Mary supported the plot and the King of France had men ready to invade if it happened. The fact that the plan had international support shows that it was a real danger, and therefore shows that there were serious threats to the life of Elizabeth.

Language shows analysis and gives a judgement about the statement in the question.

Gives a reason for judgement.

While I agree that assassination was a potential danger, the viewpoint in the statement is not valid because this was not the most important danger faced by Elizabeth. Elizabeth's spy network under Walsingham meant that neither plot really had a strong chance of succeeding. Walsingham's men found letters in code, which meant that the plotters could be arrested and executed before they could try to kill Elizabeth. Therefore, there was never any immediate danger, only potential danger. This means that other threats were more serious.

Counter-argument introduced in new paragraph.

Makes links between factors.

Key term used to show detailed knowledge of topic.

Use of detailed own knowledge.

Explains why this was a serious danger.

Links back to question.

Other dangers that Elizabeth faced were more serious than the threat of assassination, like the threat of rebellion by angry Catholics. Like the assassination plots, a main motive was opposition to Elizabeth's Protestantism. An example of this was the Revolt of the Northern Earls. This was when Northern Earls, like the Earl of Northumberland, led a march south. They wanted to force Elizabeth to accept Mary as heir. This would have divided England, as most Protestants would not accept Mary, and it would have made the assassination of Elizabeth by a Catholic more likely. It showed Elizabeth was not completely in control. There were about 5 400 rebels and even though Elizabeth raised an army of about 14 000, the revolt still lasted about a month, which shows it was a serious danger.

Sticks to the dates given in the question.

Another danger to Elizabeth was foreign invasion. This was probably the biggest danger. One example was the threat from France. For example, in 1583 there was the Throckmorton Plot, which was a plan for French soldiers to invade, remove Elizabeth and put Mary on the throne. This was similar to the Ridolfi and Babington plots, which also had French or Spanish soldiers ready to invade. Similar to those plots, this threat was created by tension between Catholics and Protestants. Because of the history of warfare between England and France, invasion was a real possibility. Invasion could have led to the execution of Elizabeth and her replacement by a Catholic monarch, which is why it was such a serious danger for Elizabeth, more than the plots to assassinate her.

Uses detailed own knowledge as evidence.

Makes links to another factor.

Explains why this was a danger.

An example that shows that the threat of invasion was a real danger to Elizabeth was the Spanish Armada. This was another danger that was influenced by Catholic opposition to Elizabeth's religious settlement. In 1588, the King of Spain formed an armada to invade England and they sailed to collect an army from the Netherlands to invade. They were defeated but this was partly due to luck for England, because of the bad weather and food that had rotted on the Spanish ships. The Armada showed that Spain and France were ready to carry out their invasions against Elizabeth, proving she was in danger.

Makes links to another factor.

Language used to show writing is analytical. Here, 'showed' makes it clear the answer is explaining why.

Signposts concluding paragraph clearly.

In conclusion, while it was true that there was a threat of assassination against Elizabeth, I disagree with the statement. This is because the plotters were arrested before they could try to kill Elizabeth, whereas other dangers were more significant. Like the plots, these other dangers were connected to the tension between Catholics and Protestants. The greatest danger was foreign invasion, because it came closest to threatening Elizabeth's life and crown. If Spain and France had both invaded, it is quite likely that Elizabeth would have lost her throne.

Gives clear judgement.

Judgement is fully justified with reasons.

A very strong answer because...

This is an analytical explanation that is tightly focused on the question throughout. It has a clear introduction, which includes a judgement. This shows the answer was well planned. The answer gives clear and accurate examples to support arguments for and against the statement, and explains them clearly. The answer is well organised and shows a wide range of knowledge, including information not given in the question. Finally, the conclusion compares the factors and gives a clear explanation for the overall judgement.

Hint

Read the notes below, then look at the sample answer on pages 47–49.

Hint

Remember – in the exam you only need to answer **either** Question 1c(i) **or** Question 1c(ii).

1c(ii) 'The main consequence of Drake's circumnavigation of the globe was to damage England's relationship with Spain.'

How far do you agree? Explain your answer.

(16 marks)

You may use the following in your answer:

- attacks on Spanish colonies
- encouraging exploration

You **must** also use information of your own.

Writing a good answer

Good answers will:

- give an analytical explanation that is tightly focused on the issue in the question throughout
- keep explanations clear and well organised throughout
- include information that is accurate, relevant and closely linked to the question
- show a wide range of knowledge and understanding of the topic
- reach an overall judgement that is justified.

Relevant points which support the statement may include:

- Anglo-Spanish relations were damaged by Drake's piracy against Spanish colonies and ships.
- Elizabeth's decision to reward Drake with a knighthood suggested she officially approved of his piracy.
- Since a previous Pope had granted Spain and Portugal the right to control the Americas, Drake's actions were seen as a direct challenge against Spain.

Relevant points that counter the statement may include:

- Drake established an English colony, Nova Albion, a success that encouraged the idea of European settlement of the Americas.
- Circumnavigation found trade routes that enhanced trade between England and China, India and West Africa, which increased the wealth and power of England.
- The achievement increased England's reputation as a great seafaring nation.
- Drake's crew returned with information about the New World, which encouraged others to explore.

Good plan helps keep answer well structured and tightly focused on question.

Hint

Look at this sample answer to Question 1c(ii). Refer back to the notes on page 46, then look to see how some of the points are used here.

Q1c(ii): sample answer

Plan:

Support	Challenge
1. Attacking Spanish colonies • Also attacked Spanish ships • Elizabeth knighted Drake 2. Nova Albion • Drake claimed a colony • Pope had given Spain and Portugal right to New World	3. Trade • China, W Africa, India • Spices, silk, gold • Slave trade 4. Confidence in English sailors • Important for Spanish Armada 5. Encouraged exploration • Drake said it was safe • Wealth – Drake brought back £500 million in today's money • New colonies
Judgement – Spanish relations more important in short term but in long term the growth of English exploration and trade led to the British Empire.	

When Drake circumnavigated the globe and returned to England in 1580, there were several consequences. I agree that the main consequence, at least in the short term, was that England's relationship with Spain was damaged. But it also opened up trade to new countries, gave English sailors more confidence and encouraged other people to explore the New World more.

The viewpoint in the statement is valid because Drake's circumnavigation of the globe clearly damaged England's relationship with Spain badly. This can be supported by, for example, the fact that Drake's crew survived by raiding colonies and Spanish ships around the coast of South America. They did this partly for supplies and partly to get revenge for a previous defeat by the Spanish. This angered the Spanish because it affected their trade and profits. Because Drake sailed for England, the Spanish blamed England. This damaged their relationship.

Introduction is kept short.

Uses analytical language to introduce a judgement.

Identifies both sides of the issue.

Paragraph starts with a very focused point.

Gives evidence and shows knowledge and understanding.

Explains why the evidence supports the view in the statement.

Links point back to question.

Shows detailed knowledge to support point.

Explains how the evidence supports point.

Key term used to show detailed knowledge of topic.

Adds another point in support of the statement.

Uses specific detail to explain the consequence.

Links point back to question.

Language used shows writing is analytical.

Clearly moves on to the counter-argument.

Shows detailed knowledge of the period.

Links back to question.

Shows how factors link together.

In addition, the relationship became worse when Drake returned to England. Elizabeth knighted him on the deck of his ship as a reward for his actions. This sent a message to Spain that Elizabeth supported what Drake had done, which damaged the relationship even more. This was part of Philip II's reason for launching the Spanish Armada. Therefore the Anglo-Spanish relationship declined further.

While Drake was circumnavigating the globe, he damaged the relationship with Spain further by claiming a colony, Nova Albion, for England in 1579. When he stopped to repair one of his ships, the Native Americans did a ceremony that he thought was a crowning, so he said that Elizabeth was queen there. But 100 years earlier, the Pope had given Spain and Portugal the right to have colonies in the New World, so this offended Spain. They thought that England was taking land that belonged to them. As a result, England's relationship with Spain was damaged further by the circumnavigation voyage.

Although I agree to an extent with the statement, at least in the short term, in the long term there were more important consequences. One was that his voyages identified routes for sailing that allowed other ships to trade with China, India and West Africa. Merchants began trading in spices from India, silk from China and, later, slaves from Africa. This trade increased English wealth and led to England developing its international trade. This was an important consequence, as the growth in trade and shipping links contributed to the development of the British Empire over the following centuries.

Another consequence was that Drake gave English sailors confidence. His crew were only the second in history to sail round the world, so people believed that English sailors were better than other sailors. This was important when the Spanish Armada attacked in 1588, as the English were confident that they were better sailors. As a result Drake's circumnavigation helped them to defeat the Spanish Armada, and therefore allowed Elizabeth's monarchy to survive.

Another consequence was that Drake's voyage encouraged people to explore and claim new land for England, which would lead to more English colonies. When he returned, he had treasure worth about £500 million in today's money and so other people wanted to get the same wealth. Also, Drake said that the Native Americans were friendly, so it seemed possible to settle and take land in the New World. Many more wealthy men started to spend money on ships and crews to sail to the New World as a result. Although the first attempts, like Raleigh's colonisation of Virginia, failed, eventually new colonies were established in the 1600s once hostilities with Spain ended. This, combined with the growth of trade to China and India, and the slave trade from West Africa, which provided workforces for growing colonies, led to the growth of the British Empire and the slave trade, which made Britain wealthy.

Overall, the viewpoint in the statement is valid to a certain extent. In the short term the main consequence was that Drake's voyage damaged Spain's relationship with England. It led to Spain's attack on England with the Spanish Armada. Until hostilities with Spain ended, England did not gain more positive outcomes like developing an empire. In the longer term though, the circumnavigation led to England starting to explore more, and this led to England becoming a powerful country. Longer term therefore, the main consequence was an increase in England's power and international importance.

Very specific details show good knowledge and help support point.

Explains why this evidence challenges the statement.

Shows wider knowledge and understanding of consequences.

Reaches a clear judgement.

Explains a sophisticated judgement about short- and long-term importance.

Clear language signals concluding paragraph.

A very strong answer because...

This answer is well organised and tightly focused on the question throughout. It gives an analytical explanation and does not just describe the story of Drake's circumnavigation. It includes accurate and relevant information, showing a wide range of knowledge and understanding of the topic. It examines evidence that both agrees with and challenges the statement. It reaches a clear overall judgement that is fully justified.

Answers

Where an exemplar answer is given, this is not necessarily the only correct response. In most cases there is a range of responses that can gain full marks.

KNOWLEDGE BOOSTER

1. Government and religion

1 Court – friends and advisers who influenced the queen's decisions.

Plus:
  - Justices of the Peace – kept local law and order.
  - Lord Lieutenants – governed English counties and raised the local militia.
  - Privy Council – helped Elizabeth to govern the country.
  - Parliament – passed laws and controlled taxes.

2

Challenge	Give **one** reason why this was a problem for Elizabeth
She was unmarried	Any one from: • Many people expected her to marry • A husband would limit her power
Her legitimacy was challenged	Any one from: • Her right to rule was questioned • Mary, Queen of Scots, could claim a right to the throne
The government had financial problems	Any one from: • New taxes would be unpopular • Armies and navies were expensive but necessary to defend England

3 Scotland; France; Spain

4 Aiv; Bi; Ciii; Dii

2. Government and religion

5

	Puritans	Catholics
Two reasons why they opposed the settlement	Any two from: • They wanted their own Puritan church • They wanted a simpler style of worship • They were anti-Catholic and opposed any aspects of the settlement that seemed Catholic	Any two from: • They saw Protestantism as heresy • The settlement reduced the power of Catholic nobility • They objected to attending Protestant church services • The Pope issued an instruction in 1566 for Catholics not to attend Church of England services

	Puritans	Catholics
One example of how they opposed the settlement	Any one from: • They opposed Elizabeth putting a crucifix in each church • They opposed Elizabeth introducing vestments for the clergy	Any one from: • Not attending Church of England services • Rebellion of the Northern Earls • Burning Protestant books • Practising Catholicism in secret (recusants)

6 Any three reasons from:
  - Elizabeth was Protestant.
  - In 1562 Elizabeth supported French Protestants in a revolt.
  - England supported Dutch Protestant rebels against Spain.
  - Elizabeth confiscated a loan of gold from Genoa to Spain.
  - France had the 'auld alliance' with Scotland who also opposed England.

7 Mary had a claim to the throne because she was Henry VII's great-granddaughter.

8

Possible solution	Potential new problem
Hand Mary to Scottish lords	They might execute her, triggering war with France and Spain
Help her to retake the Scottish throne	There would be another Catholic ruler near England
Keep Mary in England	Catholics in England might overthrow Elizabeth
Send Mary abroad	It could provoke a French plot against Elizabeth

3. Challenges to Elizabeth

1 Answers will depend on your own judgement. The key thing is to have clear reasons for the choices you make.

2 Any two from:
  - A spy network
  - Ciphers and code breakers
  - Torture
  - Execution
  - Agents provocateurs to protect Elizabeth.

3 Any four from:
  - She was involved with plots like the Babington Plot.
  - She was found guilty under the Act for the Preservation of the Queen's Safety.
  - Walsingham's spies found evidence of her plotting.

- There was a threat of Spanish invasion that could make Mary monarch
- Mary was a rallying point for English Catholics

4 Any two from:
- Executing an anointed monarch made future monarchs more vulnerable.
- The execution gave Philip II of Spain more reason to attack England.
- The succession was more uncertain, making civil war more likely.
- An important threat to Elizabeth was removed.

5 A. False – Spain and England competed for trade; B. True; C. False – Elizabeth knighted Drake as a reward for his actions against the Spanish; D. True; E. True

4. Challenges to Elizabeth

6

Event	Why this made England's relationship with Spain worse
Dudley's campaign in the Netherlands, 1585–88	Any one from: • The campaign made war with Spain a reality • England was involved in a country Spain controlled • The English prevented the Spanish capturing Ostend, which they needed
Francis Drake's raid on the Spanish navy at Cadiz, 1587	Any one from: • He destroyed 30 Spanish ships and many supplies • Philip II was humiliated and sought revenge

7 B

8 Philip II launched the Spanish Armada. The purpose was to attack <u>England</u>. A main reason for this was that Philip wanted to put a <u>Catholic monarch</u> on the throne of England. The <u>Pope</u> had promised absolution to anyone who supported the Armada.

9 B

10 Correct answers: A; C; D; E; G; H

5. Society and exploration

1(a) Using private tutors

(b) Male children of the gentry, merchants, yeoman farmers and craftsmen aged 10 to 14 years old

2 For the lower classes, any five from:
- football
- wrestling
- baiting
- cock-fighting
- theatre plays
- playing music
- public musicians
- dancing

For the nobility, any five from:
- hunting
- fishing
- real tennis
- bowls
- fencing
- literature
- theatre plays
- playing music
- private musicians
- dancing.

3 A. False – the number of people in poverty increased in Elizabethan England; B. True; C. True; D False – land for sheep meant less food was grown and fewer workers were needed.

4

Law or action	How did it affect the poor?
Poor rate	Money was spent on improving lives of the poor
Charity	Wealthy people gave money to provide foundations to help the poor
1563 Statute of Artificers	People who did not pay poor rates were punished
1576 Poor Relief Act	JPs were required to provide the poor with raw materials to work and sell
1572 Vagabonds Act	Vagrants would be whipped and have a hole drilled through each ear They could be executed for their third offence

6. Society and exploration

5 Aiii; Bi; Cv; Div; Eii

6 B; C; E

7 Any two reasons from:
- Britain's reputation as a seafaring power increased.
- New trade links and colonies were soon established in New England.
- England focused on her navy for defence and trade.
- English ships began to trade in more places.
- Relations with Spain became worse.

8 One reason from:
- He raised funds for the project.
- He persuaded people to leave England and settle in Virginia.

9 Any two reasons from:
- Shortage of food
- Poor leadership
- Lack of skills and experience
- Native American attack
- War with Spain in Europe

Notes

Notes

Published by Pearson Education Limited, 80 Strand, London, WC2R 0RL.

www.pearsonschoolsandfecolleges.co.uk

Copies of official specifications for all Pearson qualifications may be found on the website: qualifications.pearson.com

Text and illustrations © Pearson Education Ltd 2020

Produced, typeset and illustrated by QBS Learning

Cover illustration by Eoin Coveney

The right of Ben Armstrong to be identified as author of this work has been asserted by him in accordance with the Copyright, Designs and Patents Act 1988.

First published 2020

23 22 21 20

10 9 8 7 6 5 4 3 2 1

British Library Cataloguing in Publication Data

A catalogue record for this book is available from the British Library

ISBN 978 1 292 31014 5

Printed in Italy by L.E.G.O. SpA

Notes from the publisher

1. While the publishers have made every attempt to ensure that advice on the qualification and its assessment is accurate, the official specification and associated assessment guidance materials are the only authoritative source of information and should always be referred to for definitive guidance. Pearson examiners have not contributed to any sections in this resource relevant to examination papers for which they have responsibility.

2. Pearson has robust editorial processes, including answer and fact checks, to ensure the accuracy of the content in this publication, and every effort is made to ensure this publication is free of errors. We are, however, only human, and occasionally errors do occur. Pearson is not liable for any misunderstandings that arise as a result of errors in this publication, but it is our priority to ensure that the content is accurate. If you spot an error, please do contact us at resourcescorrections@pearson.com so we can make sure it is corrected.